A TUNE A DAY

FOR VIOLA.

BY C. PAUL HERFURTH.

BOOK ONE.

Exclusive Distributors:

Music Sales Limited
Distribution Centre, Newmarket Road,
Bury St Edmunds, Suffolk IP33 3YB, UK.

Music Sales Pty Limited
20 Resolution Drive, Caringbah, NSW 2229, Australia.

Order No. BM10330
ISBN 978-0-7-119-1588-6

© Boston Music Company

BOSTON MUSIC COMPANY.

PUPIL'S PRACTICE RECORD

	SEPT.					OCT.					NOV.					DEC.					JAN.				
	1	2	3	4	5	1	2	3	4	5	1	2	3	4	5	1	2	3	4	5	1	2	3	4	5
Monday																									
Tuesday																									
Wednesday																									
Thursday																									
Friday																									
Saturday																									

	FEB.					MAR.					APR.					MAY					JUNE				
	1	2	3	4	5	1	2	3	4	5	1	2	3	4	5	1	2	3	4	5	1	2	3	4	5
Monday																									
Tuesday																									
Wednesday																									
Thursday																									
Friday																									
Saturday																									

Always Record Practice Time in Minutes. All Practice Time Lost Must Be Made Up.

WEEKLY GRADE

.... NAME .... ADDRESS

.... TEL. .... SCHOOL .... GRADE

	Sept.	Oct.	Nov.	Dec.	Jan.	Feb.	Mar.	Apr.	May	June	Tests
1st Week											
2nd Week											
3rd Week											
4th Week											

E—Excellent; G—Good; M—Medium, Distinctly Above Passing; L—Low, Doubtfully Passing; F—Very Poor, Failure.

FOREWORD TO TEACHERS

IN compiling this course the objective has intentionally been not to cover too much ground; but rather to concentrate on the acquisition of a thorough musical background and a solid foundation in good viola playing. These two requisites are inseparable.

A brief section is devoted to the simpler rudiments of music which should first be thoroughly understood. Another introductory section discusses the holding of the viola and bow, since, without the correct position of the left hand, and the proper drawing of the bow, good viola playing is impossible. With this in mind, considerable material has been given for the open strings before attempting the use of the fingers.

The accurate placing of each finger should be insisted upon.

Cultivate in the pupil the habit of careful listening.

The familiar hymns and folk-songs have been selected because of their melodic interest as pieces, and because, in addition, in each appears some technical point to be mastered.

The value of learning to count aloud from the very beginning cannot be over-estimated. Only in this way can a pupil sense rhythm. Rhythm, one of the most essential elements of music, and usually conspicuous by its absence in amateur ensemble playing, is emphasized throughout. For instance, Lesson 12 emphasizes an essential step in rhythmic development.

Many teachers do the thinking for their pupils, instead of helping them to think for themselves. Insisting upon the mastery of each point will not dull their interest.

What greater joy, whether it be child or adult, than to accomplish, achieve, and gain more power.

Lessons marked "Supplementary Material" may be given as a reward for well-prepared work.

Class teaching should be a combination of individual instruction and ensemble playing. At every lesson there should be individual playing so that all the necessary corrections can be made. Never allow pupils' mistakes to go unnoticed, since only in constant correction will they develop the habit of careful thinking and playing.

A decided advantage of group-teaching is that it provides experience in ensemble playing and gives every pupil the opportunity of listening to the others, of observing their mistakes, and of hearing the corrections.

For the best results each class should not be made up of more than six for a half-hour lesson, and twelve for an hour lesson. Irrespective of the numbers, the teacher must see to it that there is individual instruction as well as general directions to the class.

Classes should be regraded whenever necessary so as not to retard the progress of the brighter students, nor to discourage the slower ones. It also acts as an incentive for greater effort on the part of the pupils.

It is recommended that every student practice forty-five minutes a day. This course provides one lesson a week for a school year.

The eventual success of each pupil depends on the regular and careful home practice, according to directions.

If possible it would be well for the teacher to keep in touch with the parents.

Grateful acknowledgment is made by the author for the assistance of many teachers under whose direction this course has been used.

C. PAUL HERFURTH
Director of Instrumental Music
East Orange, N. J.

FOREWORD TO THE REVISED EDITION

Although the outstanding success of "A TUNE A DAY" in its original form for violin has far exceeded the author's expectations, its use in many school systems throughout this country, Canada and Australia has prompted the author to consult with a number of these teachers, to discuss the possibility of improvement.

Because the material has been subjected to the routine of actual classroom teaching, it has been constantly revised and improved in the light of this experience, until in its present form it represents a thoroughly workable course of study for string class teaching.

In this revised edition the author has eliminated certain exercises for which no immediate need was necessary, and has incorporated additional material in the form of new melodies, and secondary teacher parts.

The addition of a piano book to aid the pupils in ear-training and rhythm will greatly enhance the value of this course.

C. P. H.

RUDIMENTS OF MUSIC

Music is represented on paper by a combination of characters and signs, all of which it is necessary to learn in order to play the Viola intelligently.

Characters called notes are written upon and between five lines which is called the staff

The character placed at the beginning of the staff is called the Alto or C clef.

The staff is divided by bars into measures as follows:

These measures, in turn, are equal in time value, according to the fractional numbers, time signature placed at the beginning of each piece.

The time signature indicates the number of notes of equal value in each measure. The upper figure gives the number of beats or counts in a measure, and the lower figure indicates what kind of a note has one beat, such as $\frac{4}{4}$ or **C** equals four quarter notes or the equivalent half note and two quarters in each measure; $\frac{2}{4}$ equals 2 quarter notes; $\frac{4}{8}$ equals 4 eighth notes, etc

There are different kinds of notes, each variety representing a certain time value as follows.

The count for the above would be, four to the whole note: two to each half note: one to each quarter note and one to each group of two eighth notes.

The notes are named after the first seven letters of the alphabet, i.e., (a, b, c, d, e, f, g,) according to the line on or space in which they are placed

The Alto or C clef establishes the note C on the third line, from which the other lines and spaces are named as follows:

Middle C   D   E   F   G   C   B   A   G   F

In addition notes are written upon and between short lines above and below the staff   The lines are called **leger lines**.

A   B   C   D   E   E   D   C

Compass of the Viola in the first position, showing notes playable on each string used in this book.

Line Notes   **Space Notes**

Frank **A**nd **C**arl **E**ntertained **G**eorge   **G**ood **B**oys **D**eserve **F**avors

A rest indicates a pause, or silence for the value of the note after which it is named, such as

Whole Rest   Half Rests   Quarter Rests   Eighth Rests

The end of a piece is indicated by a light and heavy line

When a section or part of a piece is to be repeated it will be shown by a double bar with two dots.

Key Signatures

The Sharps or Flats found after the Clef at the beginning of each line is called the Key Signature.

These Sharps or Flats effect all the notes of the same name throughout the piece, except when changed by a new Key Signature or temporarily by an accidental. An Accidental is a Sharp or Flat which does not belong to the Key Signature. An Accidental applies only to the measure in which it is placed.

Sharps, Flats, and Naturals

A Sharp (♯) raises the note to which it applies by one-half tone.

A Flat (♭) lowers the note to which it applies by one-half tone.

A Natural (♮) takes away the effect of a sharp or flat and restores the note to its original pitch.

The Viola and Bow

v

HOLDING THE VIOLA

Take the viola, the strings away from the body, and hold it under the right arm.

(Rest Position)

REST POSITION

(1)
Stretch the fingers of the left hand out straight, the thumb pointing up.

(2)
Place the side of the knuckle at the base of the first finger, against the lower edge of the neck, so that the back of the hand is in line with the nut, or saddle, at right angles to the strings.

(3)
Let the thumb (joint not bent) rest against the upper side of the neck about one inch from the nut. The fleshy part of the hand between the thumb and first finger must *not* touch the neck.

(4)
Bend the first finger so that its tip falls on the A string (fourth string from you) about one inch from the nut. This will vary according to the size of the violin.

(5)
With the help of the right hand, without changing the position of the left hand, raise the viola so that it rests on the left collar-bone, the chin over the chin-rest.

(6)
Bring the left elbow *well under the viola* to the right, allowing the thumb to draw slightly under the neck, the hand also turning toward the side of the neck (not touching), rounding the other fingers over the strings in position to strike. Release the right hand.

(7)
By this position of the elbow, the left shoulder is brought under the viola to give support and counteract the pressure of the chin and jaw-bone. The viola should thus be held firm without the aid of the left hand.

Things to Watch

The viola should slant about 45 degrees to the right, and at such a height that the scroll of the viola is in line with the eye. Left elbow well under the viola. The nail of the first finger (left hand) should face you. This applies to the D and A strings only. The tip of the thumb should point out. Space between under side of neck and fleshy part of hand between thumb and first finger. From the knuckles of the left hand to the elbow should be a straight line.

Holding the Bow

Take the bow in the left hand, and hold at the extreme end below the frog, in such a position that the hair is facing up and the tip of the bow is pointing away from you. (1) Place the TIP of the thumb (right hand), slightly curved at the joint, against the stick so that it touches the raised part of the frog on the stick. The joint should be about ¼ inch from the hair. (2) Allow the middle finger to curve around the stick at the first joint (from the tip) opposite the thumb. (3) Place the third, or ring-finger, next to the middle finger so that it curves around the stick at the first joint, and rests against the side of the frog. (4) Allow the first finger to rest on the stick in the first joint. (5) The *tip* of the little finger rests on the stick in a natural position. Release the left hand.

The fingers should be close together. (Touching)

Silent Exercises for the Bow

With the viola in position, place the bow on the A string at different points, i. e., at the middle (*Fig. 1*), tip (*Fig. 2*), and frog (*Fig. 3*). At each point hold the bow perfectly still for 2 minutes. Take notice of the position of arm, wrist, etc., as follows: The bow must always be at right angles to the strings, i. e., parallel with the bridge, and midway between the fingerboard and bridge. When the bow is at the point the wrist should be sunk in (very slightly) and when at the frog, should be curved up (not too much). The back of the hand always flat, and always in the same relative position to the bow. Do not allow the fingers to move on the bow-stick. When placing the bow on the strings, the stick is turned slightly towards the fingerboard, so that only the edge of the hair touches the strings. This rule varies according to the dynamic effect desired. Practice this on all strings. Notice that the elbow is slightly higher when playing on the G and C strings, but never should the elbow be higher than the hand. Raise the hand to the level of the string desired, keeping the elbow entirely relaxed. Any exertion of the upper arm muscles is very harmful to a good tone.

Fig. 1   Fig. 2   Fig. 3

Signs and Abbreviations for Bowing

⊓ means Down Bow
V means Up Bow
W.B. means Whole Bow
M.H. means Middle half of Bow

Tuning Your Viola

IT is quite easy to tune your viola with the aid of a piano, and you should learn as soon as possible. If no piano is available use a viola pitch-pipe.

DIRECTIONS

Hold the viola by the larger end between the knees, supporting it by the left hand at the neck. Strike the note **A** on the piano (see diagram), or blow it on the pitch-pipe. With the thumb of the left hand pick the **A** string to compare it with the piano. If the string sounds lower (flat) the pitch of the string must be raised by turning the **A** peg away from you with the right hand. Turn the peg slowly while picking the string with the left thumb until it sounds in unison with the piano or pitch-pipe. If the string sounds higher (sharp) than the piano it must be lowered by turning the peg slowly toward you until the pitch of the string is the same as the piano. Tune the **D** string, in the same manner as the **A** string.

To tune the **G** and **C** strings, by reversing the hands, the right hand holding the neck of the viola, plucking the strings with the thumb. The pegs for these strings will be turned by the left hand the same as you did with the **right** hand for the **D** and **A** strings.

While turning the pegs always press them **into** the holes so that they will stay in position when you take your hand away.

Tune the strings in the following order, **A-D-G-C.**

When you become more advanced you will be able to tune your viola in the *playing position.*

TAKE CARE OF YOUR VIOLA

Your viola will not sound its best, nor will your learning to play it be as easy unless everything pertaining to the instrument is kept in perfect condition.

If your viola is not a new one it should be taken to a violin repairer for all necessary adjustments. Your teacher will tell you what is needed to put your viola in good playing condition.

Always keep your viola in the case when not practicing. NEVER loosen the strings on your viola but ALWAYS loosen the hairs on the bow when not playing. Rosin the bow-hair a little each day. Never allow rosin to collect on the viola or on the bow-stick; ALWAYS keep them clean.

Take a pride in the way your viola looks as well as in how it sounds. Use good strings, and ALWAYS have an extra set in your viola -case.

FOREWORD FOR OPTIONAL LESSONS ONE THROUGH FIVE

Although the outstanding success of "A TUNE A DAY" in its present form has far exceeded the author's expectations, its use in many school systems throughout this country, Canada, and Australia has prompted the author to consult with a number of these teachers, to discuss the use of the quarter note approach.

The thinking of string teachers seems to be about equally divided between the whole note and the quarter note approach for beginning string instrument students.

In order to make the "TUNE A DAY" string class method more valuable to those teachers who prefer the quarter note approach, the author has compiled optional material for the first five lessons with this objective in mind. These optional lessons appear in the violin, viola, 'cello, and bass books, thus providing for the teaching of these instruments in one group through the class procedure.

In order to simplify the learning of holding the instrument and bow at the same time, the first lesson uses the pizzicato approach through employing open string letter names only, thus eliminating the holding of the bow and the reading of pitch names on the staff.

With this approach in 2/4 rhythm the beginner is better able to think and feel the pulsation of this marching rhythm.

The whole and half note approach remains the same as before, starting with the regular Lesson One (1) on Page 1 for those teachers who prefer this procedure.

The author believes that, with these first five optional lessons included in the series of "A TUNE A DAY", it now covers the needs of all discriminating string teachers.

C. PAUL HERFURTH.

LESSON 1
(OPTIONAL)

The Open Strings Pizzicato

Pizzicato (Pizz.) = Plucking the strings. After learning the left hand position in holding the Viola (page VI), the names and positions of the open strings should be understood. See diagram at right showing pizz. position as follows: Place the tip of the thumb (right hand) against the upper right hand corner of the fingerboard under the A string. With the right hand in this position, pluck the strings (about two inches down on the fingerboard) with the first finger.

Additional exercises for open strings G, D, A, Pizz., may be written on the blackboard.

									REPEAT SIGN	QUARTER REST
① **Pizz.**	A - A	A - A	D - D	D - D	A - A	A - A	D - D	D - D .‖	D - ♩
Count:	1 - 2	1 - 2	1 - 2	1 - 2	1 - 2	1 - 2	1 - 2	1 - 2	1 - 2

② **Pizz.**	D - D	D - D	G - G	G - G	D - D	D - D	G - G	G - G .‖	G - ♩
Count:	1 - 2	1 - 2	1 - 2	1 - 2	1 - 2	1 - 2	1 - 2	1 - 2	1 - 2

③ **Pizz.**	A - A	D - D	A - A	D - D	A - A	D - D	A - A	D - D .‖	D - ♩
Count:	1 - 2	1 - 2	1 - 2	1 - 2	1 - 2	1 - 2	1 - 2	1 - 2	1 - 2

④ **Pizz.**	D - D	G - G	D - D	G - G	D - D	G - G	D - D	G - G .‖	G - ♩
Count:	1 - 2	1 - 2	1 - 2	1 - 2	1 - 2	1 - 2	1 - 2	1 - 2	1 - 2

⑤ **Pizz.**	D - A	D - G	D - A	D - G	D - A	D - G	D - A	D - G .‖	G - ♩
Count:	1 - 2	1 - 2	1 - 2	1 - 2	1 - 2	1 - 2	1 - 2	1 - 2	1 - 2

NOT IN UNISON

⑥ **Pizz.**	A - A	A - A	A - A	A - A	A - D	A - A	A - D	A - A .‖	A - ♩
Count:	1 - 2	1 - 2	1 - 2	1 - 2	1 - 2	1 - 2	1 - 2	1 - 2	1 - 2

NOT IN UNISON

⑦ **Pizz.**	G - G	C - C	G - G	C - C	G - C	G - D	G - C	G - D ‖	G - ♩
Count:	1 - 2	1 - 2	1 - 2	1 - 2	1 - 2	1 - 2	1 - 2	1 - 2	1 - 2

Ten Little Indians

Pizz.	**2** D - D	D - D	A - A	A - A	D - D	D - D	A - A	D - D
Count:	**4** 1 - 2	1 - 2	1 - 2	1 - 2	1 - 2	1 - 2	1 - 2	1 - 2

American Folk-Tune

Piano

LESSON 2*
(OPTIONAL)
Holding and Drawing the Bow

After acquiring the feeling for holding the bow correctly (P. VII)(in the beginning this can be done much easier with a pencil) try playing on the open strings.* The right arm must be completely relaxed to permit the bow to be drawn freely.

Silent bow arm exercises: With the left hand and arm holding an imaginary Viola move the right hand and arm down and up as in actual playing until complete relaxation has been accomplished. When using the bow avoid all tension in the bow arm. ⊓ = Down Bow. V = Up Bow.

Study the names of the open strings in relation to the notes as written on the staff (see diagram above). You are now playing quarter notes (one count to each note). COUNT ALOUD.

Baa! Baa! Black Sheep**
Nursery Rhyme

Jingle Bells

*Procedure for this lesson: (1) Recite letter names in rhythm. (2) Play pizzicato counting one-two.
(3) Play using bow. The bow must be held firmly with the fingers of the right hand. Use the middle two-thirds of the bow and play with a bold firm stroke. Be careful of any tension in the bow arm.
**Piano Acc. Teacher's Manual, Page 6.

LESSON 3
(OPTIONAL)
Continuation of Open String Quarter Notes
(One Count Each)

Twinkle, Twinkle, Little Star*

Nursery Rhyme

Oats and Beans

Old English

*Piano Acc. Teacher's Manual, Page 9

Home work: Write letter names above notes on this page.

LESSON 4
(OPTIONAL)

Half Notes - Two Counts Each

A half note is equal to two quarter notes tied. When two notes on the same degree of the staff (line or space) are tied by a slur ⌣, they are to be played as one note.
USE A WHOLE BOW (W. B.) (FROG TO TIP, TIP TO FROG)

Introducing Four-Four (4/4) Time

Two measures of two-four time equal one measure of four-four time. The count for each measure now becomes one-two-three-four. One-two for the first half note, and three-four for the second half note.

* Piano Acc. Teacher's Manual, Page 4
** ,,   ,,   ,,   ,,   ,, 5
*** ,,   ,,   ,,   ,,   ,, 9

LESSON 5
(*OPTIONAL*)
Whole Notes-Four Counts Each

Draw the bow with an equality of motion in a straight line parallel with the bridge. Learn to save the bow, i.e., a fault that is very prevalent is the starting of the bow at a too rapid pace, whereby the greater part of the bow is used up before half the time value of the note has expired. Whole notes four counts, half notes two counts.

(Always count aloud and give each note its full value.) USE A WHOLE BOW (W.B.)

Whole Notes and Half Notes

DRAW THE BOW TWICE AS FAST FOR THE HALF NOTES AS FOR THE WHOLE NOTES.

Whole, Half, and Quarter Notes
Folk Song

xiv

Simplified piano accompaniments to all the exercises, scales and pieces in this book will be found in the Piano Accompaniment Book for home practice or in the Teacher's Manual. Accompaniments naturally stimulate practice thereby making progress more rapid when these accompaniment books are used.

A TUNE A DAY

On the staff

On the Viola

LESSON 1
The Open Strings

Hold the bow firmly upon the strings while counting the rests. Draw the bow with an equality of motion in a straight line parallel with the bridge. Learn to save the bow, i.e., a fault that is very prevalent is the starting of the bow at a too rapid pace, whereby the greater part of the bow is used up before half the time value of the note has expired.

The Open A-String

Whole notes four counts, half notes two counts. Use whole bow for each note, drawing the bow a little faster for the half notes than for the whole notes.

Au clair de la lune

2

LESSON 2
The Open D- String

Whole notes four counts, half notes two counts. *Count aloud.*

Marching

The Open A- and D-String

In crossing strings do not lift the bow off the string. Hold the bow firmly upon the string while raising or lowering the hand.

Merrily

3

LESSON 3
Quarter Notes and Quarter Rests

1 count, use middle half of bow. Use whole bow for whole and half notes. Give quarter notes full value.

2/4 TIME MEANS { Two counts to a measure. Quarter notes get one count. }

Baa! Baa! Black Sheep
Nursery Rhyme

Hop, Hop, Hop!
German Folk Song

4

LESSON 4
The Open C - String
(Viola and 'Cello only)
(Piano accompaniments for Lesson 4 should be transposed)

Ten Little Indians
American Folk Tune

Oats and Beans
Old English

*A Riddle
German Folk Song

* By permission of Silver, Burdett & Co., owners of the copyright. From Book one,"The progressive Music Series."

5

LESSON 5
The Open G-String

Twinkle, Twinkle, Little Star

Nursery Rhyme

The Four Open Strings
(Viola and Cello only)

Home work: Write 4 lines of open string notes, marking the name of each. Divide into measures, using whole, half, and quarter notes. Mark time signature.

LESSON 6
The Eighth Note

To be played with a loose wrist and most generally with the middle part of the bow. Play slowly at first, gradually increasing the speed until you can play quite fast. *Count aloud.* Be careful not to cut the up bow stroke too short. Use the same amount of bow for notes of equal value.

Gaily The Troubadour

Thomas H. Bayly

Lightly Row

Home work: Write 4 lines of open string notes dividing into measures, using half, quarter and eighth notes in 4/4 and 2/4 time. Mark time signature.

Note: All manuscript pages are to be used for home-work according to instructions

TEST-QUESTIONS THROUGH LESSON 6

Questions from this, and following test-sheets, will be given as a check on your home-study of preceding lessons.

Remember: The more you know and understand about the signs and symbols used in music writing. the easier it will be for you to learn how to play well.

(1) This ▭ is called? . . . .

(2) This symbol 𝄡 is called? . . . .

(3) The staff is divided by bar-lines into? . . . .

(4) Fractions at the beginning of music are called . . . . signatures?

(5) This 𝄡 4/4 is a . . . . note, and has . . . . counts?

(6) These 𝄡 4/4 are . . . . notes and have . . . . counts each?

(7) These 𝄡 4/4 are . . . . notes and have . . . . count each?

(8) These 𝄡 2/4 are . . . . notes and have . . . . count each?

(9) Lines and spaces are named after the first . . . . letters of the alphabet?

(10) This 𝄡 4/4 is a . . . . rest?

(11) These 𝄡 4/4 are . . . . rests?

(12) These 𝄡 4/4 are . . . . rests?

(13) This (♯) is a? . . . .

(14) This (♭) is a? . . . .

(15) How does a sharp affect a note? . . . .

(16) How does a flat affect a note? . . . .

(17) Name the open strings? . . . .

(18) Write (notate) the open strings? 𝄡 ▭

(19) This sign ⊓ means? . . . .

(20) This sign ⋁ means? . . . .

LESSON 7

First, second and third fingers must be perpendicular from the first joint to the tip when pressing on the strings. Keep the fingers over the strings. Do not allow the little finger to curl under the neck. Listen carefully that you play exactly in tune and give each note the proper time value.

First Finger B on the A-String
Whole tone from A to B

Little A and B March

First Finger E on the D-String
Whole tone from D to E

Little D and E March

Home work: Write 4 lines of the notes thus far studied, marking name of each, and finger used.
Divide into measures using whole, half and quarter notes; mark time signature.

10

Optional Material for Lessons 7 & 8

Now The Day is Over

J. Barnby

The Boat Song

C. P. H.

Au clair de la lune

French Folk Song

Harvest Time

C. P. H.

LESSON 8

First finger B, second finger C# on the A - String

Whole tone A to B. Whole tone B to C#
Key of A Major (F#- C#- G#)

Melody

Merrily

Melody

First finger E, second finger F# on the D - String

Whole tone D to E. Whole tone E to F#.
Key of D Major (F#- C#)

Melody

Home work· Write 4 lines of notes as before, adding the two new notes in this lesson.
Write and study the key signatures of D and A Major.
*When two notes on the same degree of the staff are tied by a slur �, they are to be played as one note.

SUPPLEMENTARY MATERIAL
HARMONIZATION FOR LESSON VIII
Quartet for four Violas

LESSON 9
On the A String

First finger B, second finger C♯, third finger D
Whole tone A to B. Whole Tone B to C♯. Half Tone C♯ to B
Key of A Major (F♯-C♯-D♯)

Learn to keep the fingers on the strings whenever possible. Rule: Never lift a finger unless obliged to. Press the fingers firmly upon the strings, but but do not allow the hand to become cramped. Listen carefully to play in tune and always count. It is not music where there is no time or rhythm.

"Have you a good position"

This sign ⌢ indicates half step, fingers close together.

On the D String

First finger E second finger F♯, third finger G
Whole tone D to E. Whole Tone E to F♯. Half Tone F♯ to G
Key of D Major (F♯ - C♯)

Home work: Write **4** lines of notes thus far studied, as before.
- - - - - Hold fingers down.

14

LESSON 10
Slurred Notes (*legato)

This sign (⌣ slur) when placed above or below two or more notes indicates that they are to be played with one bow. Great care must be given to the *equal division* of the bow.

* Smoothly—connected

The Scale

A scale is a succession of tones from a given note to its octave, 8 notes higher. The form on which all major scales are modeled is as follows.

The Natural, or C Major Scale

The ascending progression is: two whole tones, one half tone, three whole tones, one half tone. The half tones come between the numbers 3-4, 7-8.

The D Major Scale— four tones on the D string; four tones on the A string.

Play the following scale and arpéggio with different bowings as indicated; also play slurring four notes to one bow. Use plenty of bow. Play slowly at first using whole bow for each note.

Home work: Write the D Major scale 4 times, marking half steps. Use key signature, and place a sharp before the notes affected.

16

LESSON 11

Up and Down the Ladder of D

LESSON 12

The Dotted Half Note and the Dotted Quarter Note

A dot is equal to one half the value of the note it follows. A dotted half note equals 3 beats; a dotted quarter note equals 1½ beats. Use the same amount of bow for the quarter note as for the half note.

Rhythm Drills

Play the model as written. Repeat, using each variation below until the rhythm is memorized.

Drill: Count aloud each variation while clapping the hands once for each note. Repeat several times, then play on the open strings.

Home work: Write 4 lines of notes thus far studied, using different groupings of notes in 3/4 time.

LESSON 13
My First Solo Pieces
(To be memorized)

Little Waltz in G

C.P.H.

In a Garden

C.P.H.

End
Fine

To the beginning
D.C.

LESSON 14
Using the D Major Scale

French Folk Song

French Folk Song

Joy to the World

Handel

Joy to the World

Beneath Thy Guiding Hand

J. Hatton

Follow bowings carefully

TEST-QUESTIONS THROUGH LESSON 14

(1) This sign :‖: means?..........

(2) This sign ⌒ means?........

(3) Name the following lines and spaces of the staff?

1st space	2nd space ....
4th line	1st line ....
3rd space	2nd line ....
3rd line	1st space below the staff ....
4th space	2nd space below the staff ....

(4) The key of 2 sharps is? ....

(5) The key of 3 sharps is? ....

(6) This note ⟨notation⟩ has.......... counts?

(7) This note ⟨notation⟩ has.......... counts?

(8) Which finger should be used for the following notes?

C# on the A string	B on the A string ....
E on the D string	G on the D string ....
D on the A string	F# on the D string ....

(9) What note is played with the following fingers?

1st finger on the D string	2nd finger on the A string ....
3rd finger on the A string	3rd finger on the D string ....
2nd finger on the D string	1st finger on the A string ....

(10) Divide the following into measures? ⟨notation⟩

(11) Write (notate) the key signatures of D and A Major? ⟨notation⟩

(12) This sign ⌒ connecting two or more notes means?..........

(13) What is a scale? ....

(14) Write and spell the D major scale? ⟨notation⟩

(15) How many D's can you play?........ E's........ G's........

(16) Mark the count under the following? ⟨notation⟩

(17) Play the D Major scale and arpeggio from memory?........................

(18) What interval is this? ⟨notation⟩ ....

LESSON 15
Detached Notes in One Bow

Semi-Staccato

A dot placed above or below two or more notes connected by a slur indicates that the notes are to be played in one bow with a short pause between each note. The bow is simply stopped an then started again. The bow, however, must not be lifted from the strings.. A slight pinching of the stick at the beginning of each note will produce the desired effect.

Holy, Holy, Holy

Dykes

Haydn
(From the Second Symphony)

Adapted

LESSON 16

The Fourth Finger on the D and A Strings

This finger being short and weak requires a great deal of attention to make it as strong as the others. Keep the elbow well under the Viola, stretch the fourth finger and press firmly with the tip upon the string. The fingers must be pressed firmly upon the strings in order to produce a clear tone. Whole tone from D to E. Whole tone from G to A.

Old English Song

Adapted

Lightly Row

The Cuckoo

LESSON 17
The Up-Beat

Many pieces begin with an incomplete measure, usually starting with the last beat or fraction thereof. This is called the up-beat and is generally played with an up bow. The ending always completes the measure of the up-beat. Follow the bowings carefully.

Two German Folk Songs

Away in a Manger
(Flow Gently, Sweet Afton)

MELODY

Spilman

ENSEMBLE

Away in a Manger

The First Noël
Chistmas Carol

Blue Bells of Scotland
Old - Scotch - Air

German Folk Song

* Note: Place the finger on two strings at once.

-*Hold—A short curved line drawn over a dot, prolongs the time of the note.

LESSON 18

Hymns and Folk Songs embracing the different kinds of notes and bowings thus far studied.   Review the written work at the top of each page. Play the bowing and fingering as marked.

Old Black Joe

Stephen Foster

MELODY

Old Black Joe

ENSEMBLE

While Shepherds Watched Their Flocks

Arr. from Handel

Massa's in the Cold, Cold Ground

Stephen Foster

Gaily the Troubadour

Bayly

LESSON 19

(Piano accompaniments for Lesson 19 should be transposed.)

Five tones on the C String
(Viola and 'Cello only)
Open C to D whole tone; D to E whole tone.
E to F half tone and F to G whole tone.
Key of C Major

Folk Song of the Civil War

Scale of C Major
(Half tones, E to F, B to C)

Use different bowings as indicated

Auld Lang Syne

Scotch Folk Song

Home work: Write 4 lines of notes, using new notes on the C string. Ma⎯ ⎯⎯low and finger used above.
Write C Major scale 5 times marking the same as the D Major. Study new ke⎯ signatures.

LESSON 20
Five tones on the G String

Open G to A whole tone, A to B whole tone, B to C half tone, C to D whole tone

Keep the elbow well under the Viola so as to let the fingers fall straight upon the strings.

Oats and Beans

Scale of G Major

One sharp, F♯. Half tones B to C, and F♯ to G

Play the following scales and arpéggio with different bowings as indicated.

Old Folks at Home

Stephen Foster

Home work Write 4 lines of notes on the G string as before, also scale of G major 4 times. Mark half steps.

LESSON 21

Review of the different keys, rhythms and bowings thus far studied.

Annie Laurie

LESSON 22

Ensemble Playing

Pieces arranged for trio (*three parts*) and quartet (*four parts*) are given for your training in ensemble (*together*) playing, and also to prepare you for your place in the school orchestra. Tunes that you have played before in this book were selected so that you could hear the melody while playing a secondary part. Listen carefully to ALL the parts so that you keep in time and in tune (*harmony*) with them. Learn to play each part equally well so that you can take turns with the other members of your class in playing the different parts.

Twinkle, Twinkle, Little Star
(Trio for Three Violas)

Teacher, advanced student or violin class may play melody.

Arr. C. P. H.

Twinkle, Twinkle, Little Star
(Optional part for String Quartet)

Waltz from Sleeping Beauty

Peter Ilich Tchaikovsky

LESSON 23

Lightly Row
(Trio for Three Violas)

Arr. C.P.H.

Pupil

Pupil

Teacher

Lightly Row
(Optional part for String Quartet)

German Folk Song
(Trio for Three Violas)

Pupil

Pupil

Pupil

LESSON 24

Old Folks at Home
(Quartet for Four Violas)

Stephen Foster
Arr. C.P.H.

Old Black Joe
(Quartet for Four Violas)

Stephen Foster
Arr. C.P.H.

TEST-QUESTIONS THROUGH LESSON 25

(1) This sign ⌢ means?. . . . .

(2) This ⁊ is an. . . . . rest?

(3) This sign ⌢ placed above or below two or more notes means? . . . .

(4) Finger the following?

(5) Bow the following?

(6) Mark the count under the following?

(7) Name the five tones on the C string? . . . .

(8) What is the signature of C Major? . . . .

(9) Write (notate) and spell the scale of D Major?

(10) Name the five tones on the G string?. . . . .

(11) What is the signature of G Major?

(12) Write and spell the G Major scale?

(13) Finger the following?

(14) Finger the following?

(15) Write the following notes?

2nd finger on the D string	1st finger on the C string
3rd finger on the C string	3rd finger on the G string
1st finger on the G string	2nd finger on the A string
4th finger on the A string	4th finger on the C string
2nd finger on the G string	3rd finger on the D string

(16) Write the signatures of G D A and C major.

(17) How many of the following notes can you play? C...B...G...A...E...

(18) Write (notate) your answers to No. 17.

(19) Music written for three instruments is called?. . . . .

(20) Music written for four instruments is called?. . . . .